UNDERSTANDING AND MANAGING DEBT

Derrick Chandler

This book is dedicated to all who seek financial freedom

CONTENTS

Title Page	1
Dedication	3
Introduction	7
Debt: An unbearable stench	9
What is debt?	13
Categories of debt	18
FORMS OF DEBT	21
HOW DEBT AFFECTS YOUR LIFE	33
HOW TO KNOW YOU NEED HELP MANAGING YOUR DEBT	37
THE BEST WAYS OF MANAGING YOUR DEBT	41
HOW TO FIND A GOOD DEBT MANAGEMENT PROGRAM	45
HOW ASSETS AND LIABILITIES AFFECT YOU WHEN PURCHASING REAL ESTATE	52
CALCULATING YOUR MORTGAGE	55
HOW TO FIND THE BEST REAL ESTATE AGENT, LOAN OFFICER AND MORTGAGE BROKER	61
Conclusion	66
Books By This Author	67

INTRODUCTION

Debt is a dream killer. A lot of people have had to forego college, change careers, postpone getting married or buying a home, because they have a huge cloud of debt hanging over their head. Debt is a glass ceiling which has constrained the ambitions of most people. A lot of Americans believe they would still be actively engaged beyond the retirement age to make ends meet and paty off their debts. This scenario is not helped by the fact that we live in a society that encourages us to buy now and pay later. this has given a lot of us a false sense of financial security.

The economic fallout of the pandemic where millions of Americans filed for unemployment benefits just 30 days off their jobs speaks volumes about the decadence in our personal finances. This books is not a cut and dry method to ending or managing your debt. The information contained in this book would be useless if you dont apply it and have the discpline to see it through. The book educates you in various forms of debt, how to know if your life is being affected by debt and the methods through which you can manage your debt.

It is recommended especially for teenagers and millenials to read before they start off in life so that they can avoid the loopholes their parents made. It is also for those who hope to break the shackles of debt and retire happily. It is a must read for anyone hopibg to be finacially free.

DEBT: AN UNBEARABLE STENCH

Debt can be described as bringing money that you would have used in the future to the present. You move money from the future to prevent when you borrow. On the flip side, you move money from the present to the future when you save. According to the U.S. Federal Reserve, Americans owe a staggering $14.3trn in debt. Many of which may not be paid in their lifetime. 63% of Americans say they hope to keep working after their retirement. Most Americans are way behind their life insurance policy, which means in the event of their demise, their dependents may not be adequately catered for.

Student loan is the second-highest debt burden after mortgage. Total student loan debt for 2020 is $1.56trn. The average student has about $32,000 in student debt, which accumulates at 8% yearly interest. Americans collectively owe over a trillion dollars in credit card debt with the average family debt of $8,377. Almost half of the U.S. working class owes credit card debt they can't pay off each month. For every dollar spent, Canadians owe $1.77, making them the country with the highest household debt ratio at 177%. In Italy, household debt is 41.6% of the country's GDP. Other countries with high household debt in relation to their national GDPs include Germany (53.5%), Japan (58%), France (60%), U.K. (87%), United States (65%) and Canada (117%). This implies that citizens of most industrial nations are the most indebted.

The above scenario tells us that citizens of the most industrial nations are groaning under the burden of debt, with few seeing lights at the end of the tunnel. By encouraging consumerism and the ability to bring our future needs and wants to the present, the government has willingly indulged people in accepting debt as a normal way of life. It is easier to take up debt for necessities and frivolities than to obtain a loan to start up a business.

Consumer spending and debt are inextricably linked. Debt fuels consumer spending, which accounts for nearly 70% of all economic activity in the United States. The more we spend, the more we are likely to take on debt provided the conditions are suitable. Society, through a consumerist culture, encourages us to spend more than we can afford. By issuing out credit cards, mortgages, or auto loans, society tells you that it is okay to borrow to fund the lifestyle you want. The government creates an enabling environment for us to be able to borrow by reducing interest rates and taxes. Why? Because liquidity is the oil that keeps the economy working. If there is no flow of cash, the economy grinds to a halt. A rise in consumer spending and debt is seen as a sign of rising optimism about the economy. On the contrast, when there is a rise in personal saving, it is seen as a lack of trust in the economy.

Have you asked why it is debts that have less impact on our financial independence that are easier to access? Debts which are not collateralized are those which are easily accessible, and revolving are those which impact us less financially. The entry requirements required for loans that do not elevate us financially, such as unsecured loans is lower than financial elevating loans such as mortgages. It is easy to obtain a credit card (the average American owns four credit cards) and carry over debts accrued on it than it is to do with mortgages, where you need to make a down payment, and the tolerance for delinquency is lower.

Such debts, because of their revolving nature, tend to be overlooked, especially if we are earning a steady source of income. We tend to spend before our salaries before they hit our account. However, these short-term unsecured loans carry a higher interest rate which further increases our liabilities and reduces our ability to pay off.

Furthermore, these types of debts are not spent on investments or creating additional sources of income. According to a 2019 research, there has been a surge in personal debts for vacations, electronic gadgets, cars and shopping. This further stretches the economy and puts it at risk of imminent collapse.

Even though we love to sweep money issues under the carpet, the stench of our debt beginning to ooze, if we do not handle it appropriately and efficiently, we would be headed to another disaster.

Already debt is affecting life patterns and choices. People are forced to change their careers and take low paying jobs in public service jobs so that they can have their debt written off. The prospect of debt is forcing many people to forego college, thereby relegating them to low-income jobs for life. Students who hope to further their studies can't attend grad school because the law prevents students from taking out loans twice. Millennials are postponing getting married, buying a house or owning their car to free up finances to pay student loan debt. *The New York Times* found, a record 22 million millennials live at home with their parents to be able to afford payments for student loans.

Since the cards have been stacked against you in what seems like a multi-layered debt trap, how can one control his finances and reduce his debt, while ensuring that he retires debt-free and financially independent? This is not impossible but is dependent on your financial discipline and planning.

This book hopes to help you achieve your financial dream of

being debt-free so that you can achieve your life milestones, attain financial independence and retire in style. It is not a quick-fix book, but one aimed at enlightening people on the dangers of debt and how they can manage and escape debt. Before we proceed, an understanding of debt. First, you need to understand what debt is, its types and various forms.

WHAT IS DEBT?

There is no need to sugar-coat it; debt is simply money you owe. It is an obligation that requires one party, (the debtor), to pay money or other agreed-upon value to another party (the creditor), at an agreed-upon time. It is money borrowed to serve a financial need that cannot be met at the time.

Contrary to populist notions, debt is not entirely bad. Intact debt could be a useful financial tool to achieve financial independence. Debt can be used to solve emergencies or start a business. If properly used, debt could serve as a hedge against the future, i.e. to mitigate future risks by taking financial action today.

However, having debts would also mean that we are robbing ourselves from future rewards. Not to mention the stress it brings to our well-being because we are trying to make ends meet. Because most of us lack financial discipline, we are unable to match our expenses to our income levels, which is the reason we went borrowing in the first place. This puts us under financial pressure because while debts increase via interests accrued, our responsibilities also increase amidst a relatively stable income and rising inflation rates. This implies that while we struggle to pay off our debts and interests, we have to balance it with tending to our responsibilities with the same income whose purchasing power is dwindling. This is why most financial experts preach against debt unless you are investing in a business.

A key element of debt or loans is the interest rate. This is compensation offered to the creditor for taking the financial risk to lend the borrower money. Interest also motivates borrowers to make payments quickly to limit interest-based expenses. The rate of interest a particular loan attracts depends on the creditworthiness of the debtor. If the debtor has a high credit rating, a lower interest rate ensue. If it is deemed too risky to lend the borrower money or if the lender is unsure if he would get his money back, a higher interest rate is charged to compensate for the risk undertaken.

Borrowers pay interest on loans as to compensate the mender for his risk. It is the price for spending money they do not have now instead of having to wait and save up.

Other factors which determine interest rates are the level of supply and demand. If the supply of funds exceeds demand, this reduces interest rates and vice versa. When there is a rise in inflation, lenders would demand a higher interest to compensate for reduced purchasing power.

For clarification purposes, whenever debt is mentioned in this book, it refers to personal debt. This is different from corporate debt which is debt owed by corporate institutions and is beyond the scope of this book.

Consumerism And Debt: Why The Government Needs You To Borrow

If it makes sense to live a frugal lifestyle, why is debt skyrocketing? Why are more people neck deep in debt now than was obtainable two decades ago? The reality of this paradox becomes clear when we understand that debt is an intricate part of the economic system.

Globally, there is as much debt as there is money in circulation. Debt ensures that the system is liquid and guess justification for the transfer of capital. The more people borrow money, the more funds are injected into the economy. If a nation wants more money in the economy it has to go further in debt. This is why when consumer debt and mortgages rise, it is seen as an indication of an economy that is doing well.

The injection of debt creates new money which would be accessed and spent by people. This way the economy keeps flowing because of the liquidity. In countries such as the United States, whose currency is not backed by gold, the solution to the debt crises is simple- print more cash. However, this cash cannot just be dumped in the economy or Federal Reserve. There has to be a basis or justification for such money to enter into the economy. Debt provides the path through which the money can enter into the system and circulate. Let's assume everyone wants to pay his or her debt the same time, the financial system would collapse, just the way if every customer wants to withdraw their money from the bank at the same time.

The economy of most industrialized nations revolves around debt. if people are not willing to spend, how would jobs be created, good be produced, or services be rendered? The economy requires people to spend on things they do not need, but want. While governments and corporations can roll over debt or even get it outrightly wiped off through bailouts, the narrative is not the same for consumer loans which the individual must pay off.

Advertisers fuel consumerism. It is no secret that advertisers spend millions researching on the how best to induce us to spend money. By collecting online data and digital footprints, advertisers and marketers are profiling us based on our online activity to understand put tastes and preferences. Using Artificial intelligence and machine learning, companies are able to predict with a high degree of precision what our choices would be and tailor adverts which are somewhat personalized to our preferences. This allows companies position their products and services and implement smarter funnels that the consumer responds more positively.

For example, algorithms can be used to determine when you are most likely to convert i.e. buy and item. As a result, advertisers send you promotional emails to customers at prime times that generate a jump in sales. Now you know why you get those irritating emails and annoying in-app notifications.

Technology has also made us more impulsive than ever before. We are inundated by images of products and services which are available with just the flick of a finger. Customers are now more exposed to a wider array of options than ever before. Our visual spaces have been overtaken space by every kind of branded image. Plus, shopping is more convenient now. You can order, make payments online and have the goods delivered to your doorstep.

The implication is the worrisome fact that all this purchasing which has been possible by easy access to credit could be driving us into debt. Revolving loans such as credit card loans which can be carried over mean we can amass material things at levels which were not obtainable in previous generations. It is society's way of telling us that it is good to be in debt provided you have a means of income.

It is no coincidence that this conditioning starts at an early age. Credit-card companies begin soliciting consumers in high school, offering credit at high interest rates to students who have no financial experience or adequate money management skills. There are countless how-to manuals on qualifying for debt, raising credit scores and managing that first credit cards targeting young people. This behaviour expectedly follows them into adulthood and beyond, making them see debt as a usual way to solve financial problems. This explains why most people take borrow more money to offset the present debts through schemes such as debt consolidation.

Technology and advertisement may be catalysts to consumer spending, but if the macro-economic climate are not favourable for retail buying, people would be less inclined to borrow and spend money. Interest rates influences consumer behaviour which in turn spikes debt levels depending on how the pendulum swings. When interest rates are down, loans are cheaper to access and service, which invariably increases the borrowing, which leads to more spending.

On the flip side, when interest rates are high, consumers shy away from borrowing because loans become expensive to service. By tweaking interest rates, government can stimulate consumer borrowing which means more indebtedness for its citizens. Since the government needs debt to pump in more money and stimulate economic growth, it is not surprising that we are encouraged to take up debt when interest rates are low.

Infact the rise in consumer debt or mortgage is seen as a sign of positive economic activity. Because debt fuels the purchasing power of people. They can buy goods, pay for services which triggers economic activity. As people borrow more, more new money comes into the economy. All this spending is facilitated by money which is borrowed from the banks. This gives people the notion the economy is buoyant, thus providing an incentive to borrow even more. As the amount of money in circulation increases, so does debt.

An increase in personal savings is seen in a contrasting manner. Economists believe that people do not gave enough confidence in the economy and so hoard money rather than putting it in circulation. This inevitably stretches the economy as there would be less liquidity in the system.

The twist however lies in what the debt is being used for. If debt is used for capital projects and infrastructural developments, then debt would have positive ripple effects for generations to come. However, when debt is raised simply to fund public consumption, such as proceeds used for Medicare, Social Security, and Medicaid, then debt could be militating and dangerous because it does not support economic growth. This also applies to our personal finances. If we borrow to fund our lifestyle, we are setting ourselves up for more debt.

CATEGORIES OF DEBT

There are four main categories of debt. These are secured, unsecured, revolving debt and mortgages. These are treated below.

Secured Debt

Secured debt is any debt backed by an asset. This type of loan is secured against by a collateral. If the borrower defaults on his payment, the creditor can repossess the collateral and dispose of it to retrieve funds back. While the lender may carry out necessary credit checks on the borrower to ascertain his credit worthiness, the collateral in most cases is a guarantee against default in payment.

An example of a secured debt is a car loan. A creditor finances the purchase of your car in return for installment payments at an interest rate. If you default on payment, the creditor has the right to sell it to recoup his funds. Because they are backed by collateral, secure debts usually have a lower interest rate than unsecured debts.

Unsecured Debt

Unsecured debts are debts which are not backed by collateral. This type of loans are issued based on an estimation of the borrower's ability to repay the loan using income and credit history as guidelines. Examples of unsecured debt include credit cards, utility bills, gym memberships, and medical bills.

Since unsecured debts are not backed by any collateral, borrowers are motivated to keep borrowing. This also makes them less inclined to paying them off. delinquency rates on unsecured loans are high than secured loans because the customer could declare bankruptcy. As such, they come with high interest rates as compensation to the lender for his risk.

Revolving Debt

Revolving debt refers to the type of debt that is incurred on a recurring basis. They are open lines of credit which enable a customer borrow a limited amount of money on a recurring basis. It is a cycle of borrowing and paying back simply to borrow more. As the customer pays off his debt, the credit is replenished allowing him to borrow more within his limit. The process goes on like a revolving door, only in this case there is a limit to how many times you can revolve round the door (borrow). An example of revolving debt is credit card debt which allows you to borrow up to a certain amount (credit limit), and as long as you make the minimum payment by a specific date each month, you can keep spending.

One thing with revolving debt is that it gives one the illusion of financial buoyancy. This is because you only need to meet up with your specified minimum payments each month to keep revolving the debt. This can be quite misleading. Paying only the required minimum every month does not reduce interest accrued on the principal. Which implies you may be racking up more debt than you previously envisaged. In addition to this, when you default you pay more in form of penalties for late payment.

Non -Revolving Debt

A non-revolving debt is a debt that is incurred on a one-time basis. Once the debt has been paid off, the line of credit can't be used again. Non-revolving loans are usually used to finance capital intensive or long-term projects such as a business loan, a student loan or mortgage. The borrower makes monthly instalment payment over a period of time frame depending on how much you originally took out. Once you've paid the loan off, it's gone, and you don't get any more funds to spend. There is usually a penalty if you pay ahead of your schedule.

Mortgage is the most common type of non-revolving debt that people get into. Since the subject real estate serves as collateral, the interests rates accrued on mortgages are usually the lowest in consumer loan, and the interest is often tax deductible.

FORMS OF DEBT

Student Loans

Education is a fundamental human right, because it develops our citizens and makes society a better place. This rationale is the anchor upon which government hinge policies and programs aimed at ensuring that everyone has access to quality education. One of such policies is allowing people borrow to fund their post-secondary education with the hopes that they would pay back when they employed. The debt incurred by taking these loans is known as student loan debt.

Student loan debt is the second-highest category of consumer debt behind mortgages in the United States, above credit card and auto loans. According to *Forbes* magazine, about 44.7 million Americans are owing a combined total of $1.56 trillion in federal loan student debt and $119 billion in private student loans.

At an average amount of $32,731, the financial burden that comes with student loan debt exacts a crushing toll on the debtors' finances and is proving to be a hefty cost for the economy. Analysts have projected that at a growth rate of 7% a year, total student loan debt would reach $2 trillion by 2021, and as much as $3 trillion by the end of the next decade.

Student Loan Debtors By Age Group

Based on the data compiled by the United States Department of Education, the largest concentration of student loan debtors as at Q2 2019, are found within the age group 25 to 34 years-old with an outstanding debt of $454.6bn. This is followed by the 35-49 age group with an accumulated debt of $406.8bn. years of age with a total deficit of $42.8bn. The least indebted age category is those above 62.

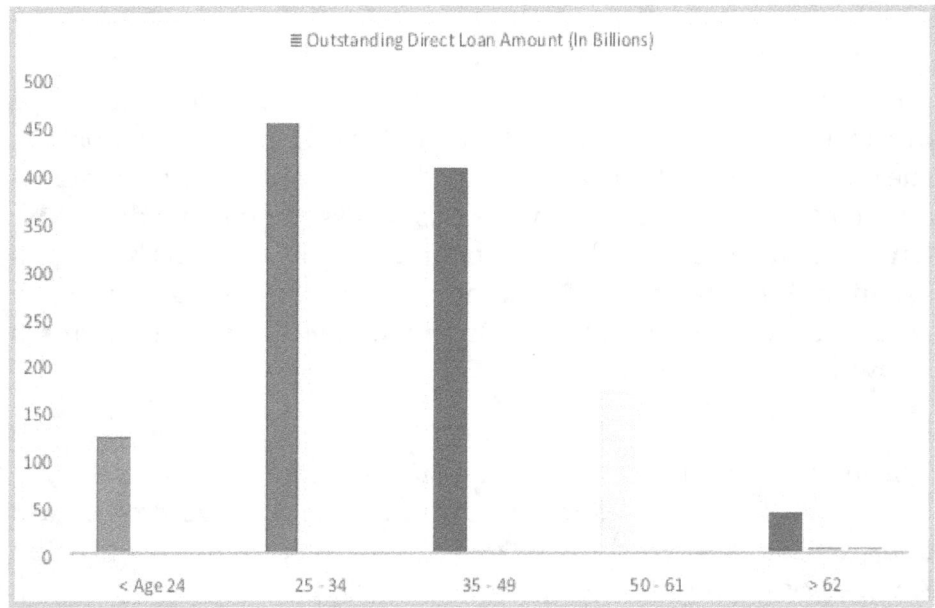

Source: *U.S. Department of Education*

Other interesting facts about student debt as compiled by the **Brookings Institute** includes

- 70% of college students graduate with student loan debt
- Only 8% of student debt owed is above $100,000
- 23% of debtors graduate with less than $20,000
- Graduate students account for 48% of all outstanding student loan debt
- Graduate students have lower student loan default rates

- Debtors that owe less than $5,000 default the most

How Student Loan Affects You

Student loan comes with tremendous burden for borrowers which could have ripple effects on their life. If not properly managed and planned for debt incurred from student loan could have life altering consequences for the borrower.

Student debt has become a major obstacles to the financial independence young people. Compared with earlier generations, millennials have higher student debt. According to the Pew Research Centre, 70% of college students graduate in debt, owing about $30,000 on the average. NerdWallet estimates the average student debt for a 2020 high school graduate at $37,200.

This huge mountain of debt has brought about a socio-economic shift in the lives of young people. *Forbes* magazine reports that millennials are now posting life milestones because they have a huge debt to consider. according to a survey carried out by finance company, SoFi, 35% of millennials saw paying off student debt as their most important milestone. A quarter of respondents said buying a home is the most important milestone, 17% believed that saving for retirement was important, 15% said starting a family, and 4% said starting to invest. Infact, paying off student-loan debt deemed so significant that people are celebrating with parties and vacations.

Fewer young people are getting married, buying a car or moving into their own homes. While most baby boomers spent their twenties building families, many millennials are postponing tying the nuptial knots or having children, citing the economy as the main reason. This lack of familial obligation has prompted many young adults to continuing living "college style" late their late twenties. Sharing apartments with roommates or living with parents is not uncommon among millennials.

More adults between aged 18 and 35 are living with their

parents, than was the case for their counterparts a decade ago. According to a survey carried out by *WalletHub,* more than 2 in 5 college graduates say they get help from their parents with their credit card tab. The Pew Research Centre reports that about 6 in 10 parents with children aged between 18 and 29 said they have offered their kids financial help for recurring expenses such as tuition, rent, groceries or bills in the past year.

Student loans have morphed into dream killers, which in essence is a paradox. The very debt that's taken to allow one to pursue their dreams and live a better life later prevents them from achieving their aspirations. to then abandon those plans and. It is a major stumbling block to the entrepreneurial aspirations of young people as many faced with burdensome student loans see a job as the only way of paying off their debt.

According to the *Harvard Business Review,* the number of startups by young people has been on a steady decline since the mid-90s. In 1996, young people accounted for 35% of startups, by 2014, this number had trickled down to 18%. 60% of student debt borrowers expect to be paying off their loans into their 40s.

This is exacerbated by the fact that wage growth has not kept pace with rising interest rates. As such, economic development is hampered because the young population, the core of a nation's innovation and economic growth are been weighed down by huge debts and as such can't take the needed financial risks which could bring about economic development.

This has also put their financial future at risk, especially when they become non-productive and retired. Many young people are not adequately saving for their retirement., hardly their fault when you consider the pile of debt they have to contend with. Though other factors such as age and financial recklessness take their share of the blame.

Until recently, the government believed that student loan would be profitable. However, after a revision on a prior estimate carried out by the Congressional Budget Office, it was discovered that student loans cost American tax payers a whooping $307 billion, upwards from the Congress' estimate of $31billion. This implies that the effect of student loan debt is already is costing tax payers more money than previously. Monies which would have been diverted to other critical sectors such as health is being used to service student loans.

How To Pay Off Student Loan Debts Faster

Much as we all deserve quality education, we don't want the cost of educational aspirations to robs us of our much-deserved financial independence in the future. Having a student loan which spans as much as 30 years can be frustrating and limiting. As such, we need a framework or strategy to enable us to pay off student loans without denying ourselves future benefits. You can try or combine any of the tips below to allow you to pay off your student debt faster.

Refinance Or Consolidate

Refinancing or consolidating your student debt is one of the ways that you can pay off your student debt faster. They are essentially the same process but differ in terms of who the lender is. Student loan refinancing is when you obtain a loan from a private lender to pay off one or more existing student loan.

Debt consolidation on the other hand is combining federal student loans with other loans (except state or private loans) into a single Direct Consolidation Loan. This new single student loan comes with a single monthly payment typically ranging between 5 to 20 years and lower interest rates, which may be fixed or variable. You can only refinance through private lenders, while you can only consolidate federal loans.

Loan service providers usually evaluate your credit profile by looking at your income, monthly cash flow and other factors. There are various ways to consolidate your debt. This is treated in the section that deals with debt consolidation. Try using a student loan refinancing calculator to find out how much you can save when you refinance student loans.

Increase Payments On Your Student Loan

Another smart way of reducing your student loan debt is by increasing your monthly payment. The quicker you reduce your principal, the less interest rates you pay off your loan, which means less overall costs. One loophole most people fail to exploit when it comes to student loans is that there is no prepayment penalty. This means you can pay off your student debt early without attracting any form of penalty.

Let's assume you owe $100,000 of student loans at an interest rate of 8%. Your monthly remittance is $1,113. If you decide to increase your monthly payment by $200, which brings your new monthly remittance is $ 1,226. The extra $200 payment will save you over $11,000 over the duration of the student loans and help you pay off your student loans earlier by as much as a year.

You could also make a lump payment. If you got extra cash through a bonus, tax refund or gift, you can use such money to pay your student loan debt. Just make sure you inform your student loan servicer to apply such payment to your principal.

Choose Your Pay-Off Date

Having the discipline to pay off debts is more psychological than financial. You can choose a stipulated time at which you would pay-off your student loan. Having a designated timeframe keeps you focused on your debt reduction goals and helps to evaluate your progress towards its achievement. Plus, you begin to see every income generated as a potential debt reducer. It helps you live a more frugal lifestyle which is key to achieving financial independence and building wealth.

Get into public service

One of the easiest ways of getting your student loan wiped off is getting into public service, if actually you do get in. The establishment of the Public Service Loan Forgiveness program in 2007 cancels all federal student loans for people in working in federal, state, local or non-profit organizations. Provided you meet the specified criteria, you can have your federal student loans cancelled after making monthly payments for 10 years.

Get a side hustle

While off debt means that you have to earn some extra income to reduce the financial pressure on your current income. Paying off student loan debt involves extra money. As such, you need to double-up on your hustle to bring your student debt reduction plans to fruition. Getting a side gig is the been the rule of thumb when it comes to earning extra income. way of earning extra income which can be used to offset your student loan debts. The possibilities are endless, especially in a growing gig economy where you can work from just about anywhere and earn money. You can also take up part-time jobs to raise the much-needed extra cash.

Prioritize payments by interest rates

Prioritizing payments by interest rates, i.e. pay the high-interest balances first, is another smart way of reducing your student loan debt. This way, you reduce the overall amount that you would pay because you tackle the loans that accrue the most interest first. Rank your student debt by interest rate then start by paying the one with the highest interest rate, then move over to the next in the ranking. When making extra payments, you can use this process until your debts are paid off completely.

Make bi-weekly payments

If you can also choose to pay your student loans every two weeks. You can split your monthly payment into half and make payments every two weeks. This reduces your interest rates since interest on student loan accrues daily. It also helps mentally because amount been paid is smaller, which is easier to deal with psychologically.

Credit Card Debt

When you purchase an item that you can't pay for through a card system, the debt incurred refers to credit card debt. It is an accumulation of a client's outstanding balances owed to the card company. The debt can be carried over on a revolving basis provided minimum monthly payments are met.

Credit cards don't seem like big of a deal at first. Your paycheck can't cover those emergencies, because you are low on cash and high on responsibilities. Credit cards could be a life saver in such desperate situations. However, after a while, the debt begins to pile up, and minimum payments become harder to pay off. Before you realize it, you've got $10,000 of debt and an empty bank account.

In the United States, credit card debt has been on the rise since the wake of the Great Recession. So has credit card ownership. Low restrictions on credit card ownership have made it easy to open and maintain numerous credit card accounts with varying terms and credit limits. More than 189 million Americans have credit cards, with the average wallet holding at least four cards.

The revolving nature of credit card debt - means that debts can be carried over monthly, provided you pay the minimum amount. As such, people tend to spend beyond their means, thereby piling up debt. Interest rate on Credit card debt is are the highest, and there are penalties fir defaulting.

Data released by the Federal Reserve in 2019 stated that Americans collectively owed over a trillion dollars in credit card debt. The average American family is indebted by $8,377. The increase in credit card debt has led to a spike in delinquency rates. In 2019, the Federal Reserve reported a rise in credit card delinquencies of 30 days or more, after tapering off for years. This implies that more people are defaulting on their credit card payments leading, a trend which is seen as evidence of an economy that isn't doing well.

Dangers Of Credit Card Debt

Credit cards could cut both ways if misused. Though they could be helpful, but also harmful to our financial well-being. The lure of buy now and pay later entices people to spend more than they can afford. The illusion of "free" money by just swiping your credit card make people get reckless with their spending, accumulating items they do not need. If you are flirting with the idea of getting a credit card, having an understanding of the financial pitfalls that may be involved could help you develop better money management skills.

You spend more

Due to their revolving nature of the debt, we tend to be less cautious when making purchases through their credit cards.

Also, because we don't physically see the money we are spending, the reality of our spending does not set in immediately. When that laptop you've had your eye on costs $1,000, you think long and hard about it. But when you see that you can buy it for $42 monthly spread over 24 months, it suddenly feels a lot more affordable.

Studies have shown that people spend up to 100% more when

using their credit card to pay than when paying with cash. McDonald's once reported that when people used credit cards, its average ticket was $7, as against $4.50 when people paid in cash. When using credit cards, we are more concerned with the momentary happiness that comes with the purchase. This is why it is difficult to keep track of your spending when you have multiple cards.

Increases time you spend in debt

Due to their high interest rates, the time used in paying off credit card debt could be longer than other loans. As interest on the loan accrues, the total amount paid on the principal also increases. Also, if you miss payment, this comes at a high interest rate. The increase in numbers could have a strong psychological effect in terms of how we view the debt.

The figure from the accrued interest may seem like a mountain too high to climb over, so we tend to default. Not paying your credit card balance in full, implies that whenever you pay a portion goes to service the interest, thus increasing the time it would take to pay off your balance.

Affects your credit rating

Your credit rating suffers when you incur credit card debt, plunging further downwards when you miss payment. Credit scoring models used by lenders evaluate credit card activity when determining your credit score. This is because unlike other types of loans such as mortgage or student loan, you have more discretion with how you manage credit. As such, credit card provides an insight into your money management characteristics. How you handle your credit card accounts helps lenders access what type of risk you pose to lender through the credit scoring model.

Once you are tagged as a serial debtor, you credit rating plummets. It gives the impression that you are a high-risk customer, and as such finance organizations such as insurance companies may bill you higher when taking out loans with them. To maintain a high credit rating, you need to keep your account balance under 30% of your available credit limit. Most finance professionals would advise keeping your credit utilization to the barest minimum.

Auto Loans

Access to a car is regarded as a necessity- well, just what the government wants us to believe. Decades of policy bias towards of car-centric transportation which has resulted in neglect for public transportation has millions of Americans fully dependent on cars for their daily commute. Urban development plans which ensure that residential areas are only accessible by car, taxation policies and meager support for other modes of transportation — have increased car dependency in alarming proportions.

Car ownership does not come cheap, and often requires taking on debt. Since the end of 2009, auto loans have increased by 75%. Americans owe a combined total of $1.2 trillion in auto loan debt with an average of $18,500 per person.

A significant share of car loans is incurred by people with bad credit profiles. This makes them are vulnerable to predatory loans which are usually inflated and have high interest rates. Since a car is needed to hold a job, and with many people having bad credit profiles, there is little wonder as to why people plunge themselves further into the vicious cycle of indebtedness by signing up for bad car loans.

Dangers of Auto Loans

The rising rate of auto indebtedness has raised concerns surrounding the financial future of millions of households. It also brings to the fore the inefficiency of a car-dependent transportation system. Below are the disadvantages of auto loans.

Depreciates in value

When you purchase a car, you are purchasing an item which depreciates in value the moment the car leaves the auto shop. This means you are borrowing to acquire an asset that loses value daily. This is the start off of a vicious cycle considering the fact that interest rate rises and if you want to trade the car off, you can't use the money to offset the balance of your auto loan.

Interest Rates Can Be Higher

Interests accrued from auto loans can be higher since the no collateral is needed to secure this loan. Depending on your credit score, your interest rate could be higher or lower, but generally because auto loans are not collaterized, the lender has to charge a high interest rate to compensate for the risk of loaning you money. This makes the borrower pay more in overall total.

May affect your credit score

Like all forms of debt, auto loans have can affect your credit score, which may influence your chances of getting other forms of loans. If a borrower defaults on payment, it could plummet his credit rating downwards, negatively impact his or her credit profile.

HOW DEBT AFFECTS YOUR LIFE

Living a financially independent life is what many of us wish for. We all want to have a good home, go on vacation, send our kids to the best colleges, and retire with adequate finances. One major factor that would enable us achieve these things is money. Without adequate finances, it is challenging living a satisfying life in this modern age.

However, a recurring stumbling block that prevents us from actualizing our dream of a fulfilled life is debt. The effect of debt transcends beyond our finances, to other areas of our life. For many people, debt is like an illness that never ends but permeates every aspect of our social being. Debt causes suffering and pain to the debtor and those around him.

This inevitably affects not only how we view our existential realities but streamlines our life choices, thereby affecting the quality of life we live. If debt with its mitigating effects are not handled appropriately, it could also affect the life of our dependents and beneficiaries. A study revealed that student loans are preventing millennials from achieving milestones in life, such as getting married or purchasing a home, thus making them put their dreams on hold. Debt affects us in more ways than one. Let's have a look at the various ways that debt affects our lives.

Debt affects your physical health.

Debt can be retrogressive to your physical well-being because it induces stress. According to a 2013 study conducted at Northwestern University, researchers discovered that those who felt overwhelmed by debt had instances of high blood pressure. Findings from the survey further revealed that a higher debt-to-asset ratio was associated with higher stress levels, severe depression, poor physical health, and high blood pressure. These findings are the first to scientifically link debt to one's health status, thus laying credence to the assumption that there is a correlation between high debt and poor physical health.

Debt affects your mental health

There are many studies which have linked debt to mental well-being. A survey conducted in 2015, published in Social Science & Medicine found a link between student borrowing and the mental health of young adults. The report associated student loan with poor psychological functioning. The conclusions of this study were further validated by a separate study published in the Journal of Consumer Research which showed that perceived financial well-being is a key predictor of overall well-being. This implies that feeling good about one's finances is an essential factor in mental health.

Debt affects your social relationships.

Money is a double-edged sword which can work for or against you. When there is a mountain of debt to handle and too little money to go around, this can cause severe strain in your social relationship. Money is one of the vehicles we use to fulfil our social obligations to those around us. When you are not forthcoming in your social obligations, this could create a misunderstanding between you and your loved ones. The fact that finance has been the reason for many relationships have hit the rocks is a testament to how debt can influence our social lives. One in four indebted people say debt has hurt their relationships. Debt is the cause of many arguments between partners, creating a toxic environment of mistrust, communication breakdown and blame.

Debt can make you sleepless.

A lot of people are losing sleep because of their debt situation. According to the American Psychological Association's 2017 Stress in America survey, one-third of Americans admitted losing sleep over debt, while 62% said their financial state was a common source of stress. Poor sleep patterns have pernicious ramifications for our physical and mental health. It is a sure sign of depression and can lead to heart attack, diabetes or obesity.

Debt affects your life choices.

Debt has made people put off achieving life milestones like buying a car, getting married or purchasing a house. Debts like student loans have forced people to enter into low-paying careers in public service so that they can have their debt written off. This is particularly alarming, especially when you consider the fact that the reason why people accumulate student debt is to find their college education which is supposed to give them a shot at a better life. Paradoxically, the prospect of debt has also made people forego college education altogether. The typical undergraduate accumulates $30,000 in student loan debt. When this amount is factored in, some people prefer to forego college outrightly. This implies that they can't attend grad school and as such, reduce their chances of a high-paying job. Even those that attend college also have their chances reduced because students who leave their undergraduate programs with significant amounts of debt often cannot afford to take out another. This shows that debt may be the most significant factor hampering the progress of millennials.

Debt stifles financial independence.

This most apparent effect of debt in our life is not being financially independent. Being riddled with debt means that you have less to save and invest. The high-interest rates accrued from debt, including the implications for your credit score and debt-to-income ratio reduces your chances of being financially independent. For example, if you have a business idea but lack the funds, your credit score is a factor that lenders use to determine your loan eligibility. If this is low as a result of debt, this implies that you would have no funding for your business idea and by implication, fewer chances of being financially independent.

Debt could disqualify you from a job.

Your debt profile could be the reason you did not get that job despite doing being qualified. According to a survey carried out by CNN, companies frequently conduct credit checks as part of background checks on prospective employees, especially if you're applying for a position in the financial industry. Findings showed that 34% of companies surveyed performed credit checks on some job applicants, while 14% said they conducted a credit check on everyone who applies. This implies that if you default in your loan payments, it could be a red flag to your prospective employer.

Takeaway

Debt can have many impacts on a person's life. It can negatively affect your credit score or prevent you from buying your dream home or even renting an apartment. Debt can have a significant negative impact a person's mental health. The scenario depicted above shows that debt could have pernicious effects than span beyond our finances to affect every aspect of our life, including our future. One sure way to hedge against this is having better control of our finances. This can be achieved through appropriate money and debt management skills.

HOW TO KNOW YOU NEED HELP MANAGING YOUR DEBT

Many consequences come with living in a society like ours, where debt is seen as the norm; it is not hard to fall into the debt trap. Data shows that more Americans are living in debt now than three decades ago. With household consumer debt rising, and student loans making people postpone mortgage and marriage plans, there is little cause to doubt the influence of debt on our personal life choices. Being indebted means your financial power is reduced because you are taking money away from other areas that can be used to build wealth and plan for the future.

Yet money is an issue many of us choose not to talk about freely. It is one of the most closely guarded secrets. Most of us do not feel uncomfortable talking about money, albeit without tension. We like to maintain the aura of financial freedom, so we borrow to hide our money problems. But the reality is that our heart skips when we remember how much we owe. Most times, we choose not to remember at all because the reality of our financial situation is a nightmare many of us do not want to face. However, it is hard to keep the stench of debt from oozing on our finances. Money problems can only be hidden for a little while because it is a full circle that always catches up.

Having a grip of your debt is very crucial in achieving financial independence. Following up on our debt is one of the sound financial decisions we would ever take. This would enable us to plan our finances better and focus on what we need, and not what we think we want.

Signs that you need help managing your debt

Since we are bound to treat money emotionally rather than logically, it is quite challenging accepting when our debts have reached a critical point. To avoid getting into a precarious situation where our debt determines our predisposition, there are warning signs to look out for which would indicate that we need help in managing our debts, and help you remedy your debt problem faster.

You never have enough savings.

One way to know if you are flush is the amount of disposable income available to you after you have settled all your debt. If your debts are up, this leaves little for savings, which can plunge you into further debt when a significant financial setback occurs like losing a job or having car problems.

You only make the minimum payment on your cards.

Having too much debt means that you are operating on a tight budget, so you scalp for money. This includes making minimum payments on cards. This keeps you further in debt because you not only incur interests making you pay more money, but you also incur more expenses because responsibilities keep rising over time.

Your credit card is maxed out.

If your credit card is close to, or over the limit, it means that you have troubles managing your debt. Maxing out your credit card means that you are having difficulties controlling your expenses which is causing you to take up more debt. Even worse is having multiple cards maxed out.

Your debt-to-income ratio is high.

Checking your debt to income ratio is a sure way of knowing your financial status and how indebted you are. This is the financial tool that lenders and finance institutions use to evaluate your financial situation before issuing you any loan. It is a good litmus test to ascertain where your debt stands in relation to your income. If you have a high debt to income ratio, this is an indication that you have debt problems which you need to address. You can calculate your debt-to-income ratio by adding your monthly debts and dividing by your monthly gross income.

You are denied credit.

Credit card companies and lenders want to be assured that you have a strong likelihood of paying back your debt. A sure sign that your debt situation is critical is when lenders refuse to loan you more money. This implies that your credit score has dropped, which has reduced your likelihood of paying back a debt.

When you default

Defaulting on loan repayment is the most telling sign that you need help with your debt. This implies that you have missed a payment. This has severe implications for your credit score and could lead to forfeiture of assets if not adequately handled.

You take new loans to pay old ones.

Many people think that the best way to get out of debt is by taking a new debt to pay an old one. There is even the opportunity of consolidating our debt which comes with a lower interest rate and the simplicity of making a single monthly payment. However, taking on more debt implies that your income cannot offset your present debt. Taking up on more debt is merely buying time to repay the debt, as the amount owed is still present. This reduces our hampers of being financially independent because it reduces the ability to save and invest for the future. Taking on new loans such as home equity loans to offset od debt is riskier because you could lose your house if you are unable to pay

Debt collectors call regularly.

It's hard to find peace and tranquillity within ourselves when you are inundated with calls from debt collectors. The pressure is not something we would be able to take, which could force us to make rash decisions that could further worsen our financial situation. Plus the constantly checking up means that you have to put our plan on hold or on short-term because you have a debt collector on your neck.

You overdraw your bank accounts.

This is similar to taking new loans to pay old ones. Frequent overdraft on your account is an indication that suggests that you have difficulties managing your debts. Overdrawing on your account incurs extra charges from the bank which further pushes your finances into a precarious situation.

THE BEST WAYS OF MANAGING YOUR DEBT

Debt is the engine that ensures the liquidity of our economic system. Without debt, the government would not be able to inject money into the economy, businesses would not be able to operate, and individuals may not be able to spend. In fact, a rise in some types of debt, such as a mortgage or consumer debt is an indication that the economy is doing well. This is why we are encouraged to amass as much debt that our income can carry.

However, the seduction of easy money can be entrapping. Many people are unable to achieve their financial goals or secure their future because of mounting debt. The American society is being heavily burdened by debt with consumer debt reaching astronomical levels. More Americans are in debt, with many more saying they do not know if they can repay their debts in their lifetime.

It is always easier to deny that we have a debt problem than face it. This is why many people take up on new debt to cover their dismal financial situation. However, the most appropriate way of dealing with a debt situation is taking immediate action. This is painful and requires a lot of discipline, but it is worth the effort if your finances are important to you.

This scenario calls for appropriate measures to be taken towards managing debt. Getting a grip of our financial life entails seeking out the best alternatives to reduce or eliminate our debt. Once you have control of your debt, your financial future looks brighter because you can plan, save and invest. Let us examine the ways through which you can manage your debt.

Don't create more debt.

One effective way of breaking the cycle of debt is to stop creating new debt. This entails living with your means and tailoring your bills to suit your income. Live a frugal lifestyle and reduce your expense. Not creating more debt may not get you out of debt in the near term, but it would prevent you from incurring more costs through interest rates.

Keep an eye on your DTI.

Keeping an eye on your debt-to-income ratio gives you a realistic picture of your debt profile which allows you to manage your debt in better ways. Your debt-to-income ratio is the financial tool that lenders use to evaluate your eligibility for loans. By keeping track of your DTI, you would know when the weight of your debt in relation to your income is becoming burdensome and take appropriate steps. It helps you to reduce expenses or any spending, which would further inflate your debt.

Debt repayment program

Another useful strategy for managing your debt is by setting up a debt management program. You can set up a **debt management program** through a **credit counselling** agency. This shows creditors that you're serious about cancelling your debts. Debt repayment plans improve your credit score and help you avoid stressful financial situations such as a bankruptcy.

Prioritize your debts

Prioritizing debts by interest rate is an effective way of managing your debt. You tackle the debts that have the highest interest rates first, then scale down. This reduces overall interest you would pay on the total amount you owe. It also fast tracks your progress towards getting out of debt.

Consolidate your debt

Another way to manage your debt is to consolidate them. Some of us may feel overwhelmed by the number of creditors we need to pay each month. Plus these come at different interest rates which are sometimes challenging to keep up with. By consolidating your debt, you do not aggregate your debt into a single monthly payment but pay a lower interest rate. Consolidating loans helps to prevent default or bankruptcy.

Increase your monthly payment

Increasing your monthly allocation, which goes to service your debts, is a good strategy. This reduces the timeline for interest to accrue, which invariably means you pay less in the long run. It takes a massive chunk off your debt and makes you get out of debt sooner.

Increase your investments.

This may seem somewhat counterintuitive because you already have a debt hanging over your head and as such, your resources should go into reducing it. However, by investing, you increase your streams of income which means you have more money available to tackle your debt. While this may seem stressful in the beginning because you would be stretched thin between making your monthly payments and keeping extra change for your investment, in the long term, it tends to pay off. It also increases your credit score and reduces your debt-to-equity ratio.

Increase your income

Having an extra stream of income is a relief. This means you have more money to service your debt. You can increase your income by taking a second job, renting out part of your property, or investing in various assets.

Ask for a lower interest rate

Higher interest rate keeps you in the treadmill of debt and decreases your chances of paying off your debt. By negotiating fr a lower interest rate, you stand a better chance at managing your debt. Negotiate with your creditors for lower interest rates. Alternatively, you can Look out for promotions that enable you to pay a lower interest rate.

Owing is a choice

Even though debt gets shoved down our throats through the allure of buy now and pay later, projected by the media and advertisers that paint a glamourous picture of consumerism, you have to remember that it is you who decides to take up the debt. It is possible to use credit cards and stay out of debt. The key is being financially disciplined and going for only those things we need. This does not mean we can't enjoy the pleasures of life, but only if we can afford it. Remember, a debt essentially means you want to use your future money now. Incurring debts robs you of your financial future.

Your Best Bet Out of Debt

Most people get into debt because they adopt lifestyles that their income cant support Money management is 80% behaviour and only 20% math. If you don't control, your behaviour towards money and finances, you would never be able to address your debt problem effectively. The best way to get out of debt is by paying them off, not consolidating them. To do this, you need to change the way you view money and your debt situation. This takes a lot of discipline and sacrifice, but it is worth your while.

HOW TO FIND A GOOD DEBT MANAGEMENT PROGRAM

The humongous debt collectively owed by Americans is the worst kept secret. The number of Americans who are in debt has reached high proportions. Consumer debt is at an all-time high. A lot of millennials can't achieve their life milestones because of the financial dark hole created by student loan. Delinquency rates on credit cards are also on the rise. All these indicate how deep debt has permeated our economy and personal finances.

Yet a lot of people or economies would not be able to function effectively without debt. With a growing number of people depending on debt to take care of their responsibilities and finance their future plans, it is imperative that the government sets up an emergency plan to help its citizens from so king further into debt.

One of these interventionist plans is the Debt Management Program (DMP). This is a program that allows debtors to pay off your debts at rates that are affordable to them. Debt management programmes come as part of the debt consolidation package, which is designed to help people regain control of their finances while reducing unsecured debts. Under a DMP, your debts are aggregated into a single monthly payment at a reduced interest rate.

<u>Points To Remember When Enrolling</u>

- It takes 36 to 60 months to offset debts
- You may qualify for lower interest rate and m and

monthly payment on your debt.
- The programme rolls several debts into one payment.
- You may be restricted from using your credit card or applying for another loan while enrolled in the plan.
- Missing a payment can derail the plan and jeopardize your interest rate cuts.

Are DMPs Good or Bad?

Most people view debt management programs as a panacea to their mounting debt. This is because the credit counselling agency is seen as an organization that wants to protect the interests of the debtor through their low-interest rates and reduced payment schedules. However, not all experiences with debt management programs have been rosy. Though they present themselves as non-profit organizations, some credit counselling agencies come with hidden charges. Some others have argued about the efficacy of debt management programs, especially when there are other debt-relief alternatives such as debt consolidation loan and debt settlement program.

However, there are always two sides to an argument, and depending on which side of the fence you are on, there may be a valid reason to support your argument. The crux is that debt management programs are useful and needed. However, there are still shady organizations that dangle the promise of financial independence. As such, it begins on the consumer to conduct a diligent search to find an appropriate credit counselling agency that would help him meet his financial goals.

How To Find One That Suits You

So how do you find a good debt management program? Below are some steps which could help you during your search.

Decide what you want to achieve

Before reaching out to a credit counselling agency, it is important you clarify what financial goal you intend to achieve. This allows you to know if you need a debt management program and if you have the discipline to stick with the plan. Financial goals such as simple budgeting, are offered for free by credit counsellors, but specialized ones such as debt management, bankruptcy counselling or managing student loans, may come at extra costs.

Find a reputable credit counselling agency.

Financial issues are serious matters and as such, have to be treated with utmost diligence. The credit counselling agency you choose can make or mar your debt management plans. The credit counselling agency you choose should be organized, remit payments promptly, offer vital financial education and consumer support. If an agency does not meet these requirements, strike it off your list and look for another. Conduct a background check on the company and track reviews from previous or existing customers. This helps you gauge the agency's reputation know and to know if there are any hidden fees available.

Two reliable resources for finding credit counsellors are the National Foundation for Credit Counselling **(NFCC)** and the Financial Counselling Association of America **(FCAA)**. Alternatively, you can use the search tool of the U.S. Department of Justice to find a reputable credit counselling agency.

Go for non-profit agencies.

Most credit counselling agencies are non-profit organizations. However, there are quite a few that charge fees. Some for-profit agencies make outrageous claims by promising quick fixes for your credit and debt. Some of them operate predatory programs that offer short-term solutions but end up hurting your finances in the long run. Do not be misled. It is advisable to limit your search to non-profit agencies since the goal is to manage your debt not incur more.

Review the terms of your plan

A debt management program is a long-term relationship. This requires a thorough understanding of what that the program entails. Before starting a plan, you need to understand the terms of your repayment plan. Make sure you know how much money you would pay each month and for how long. Ask questions about fees charged by the agency and penalties for defaulting or dropping out of the program if different agencies to see which one best suits your financial goals. If you foresee problems in the future, it is best that you do not enrol in the programme.

Is Debt Consolidation Right For You?

Debt consolidation implies using different forms of financing to pay off other debts and liabilities. It is the act of taking out a new loan to pay off existing liabilities and debts. By doing this, you aggregate your various liabilities into one single debt.

Debt consolidation doesn't erase the original debt but transfers a consumer's loans to a different lender or type of loan. People prefer to consolidate their loans because it provides the convenience of servicing only one loan with and a lower overall interest rate.

 Most debt consolidation loans are offered from lending institutions and secured as a second mortgage or home equity line of credit. These require the individual to put up a home as collateral and the loan to be less than the equity available.

However, an important question that bugs most people seeking ways of managing their debts is if consolidation their debts is worthwhile. To answer this, you may have to consider the advantages and disadvantages of debt consolidation.

Some Hard Truths About Debt Consolidation

No guarantee your interest rate will be lower.

Though the interest rates of debt consolidation loans are usually lower, this is not cast in stone. Lowering your interest rate at the discretion of the lender or creditor who determines how 'low' your interest rate would be. This ultimately depends on your credit history.

Interest rates can change.

One factor people tend to overlook is that interest rates can change over time. This is especially true when you apply for "special" low-interest deals or during holiday deals. These low-interest rates are used to entice customers and applicable only for a certain period after which the interest rates could revert to their original rates. Be wary of debt consolidation plans that are offered during the holiday season as companies know that holiday shoppers tend to overspend.

You would be in debt for an extended period.

Debt consolidation keeps you in debt for a more extended period, which ultimately defeats your debt management goal in the first place. The interest rates are lowered not because you aggregated your debts into a single account, but because the period has been extended.

Debt consolidation doesn't mean debt elimination.

Debt consolidation means that you are restructuring your debt. It does not eliminate your debt.

It doesn't change your financial behaviour.

While it may address your financial predicament, it doesn't reach the root of the problem, which is your financial habit. This is why people fall back into debt even after taking out debt consolidation loans. If you haven't established good money habits, then you would most likely end up in debt again.

When Debt Consolidation is Smart

The reason why you are consolidating your debt in the first place is to ease the burden of your previous debts. However, unless you are prepared to make sacrifices and attitudinal changes towards your finance, then debt consolidation may only reinforce your vicious cycle of debt. Making changes to your spending habits is the first step. This implies reducing credit card expenses or putting them away totally. Also, ensure that your total debt (excluding mortgage) does not exceed 40% of your gross income. Pay attention to your cash flow. If it consistently covers payment towards your debt, then debt consolidation should not be a big deal.

When Debt Consolidation Isn't Worth It

Consolidation is not a one-size-fits-all solution for your debt problems. There are numerous alternatives you can consider and compare to debt consolidation. However, there are certain situations in which it may be retrogressive to apply for debt consolidation.

- If your debt burden is small or can be paid off between six months and a year at your current pace, then you do consolidate your debt.
- If your total amount of debt exceeds more than 50% of your income, and the calculator above reveals that you do not need to consolidate your debt, then you are better off seeking other alternatives such as debt relief
- If you are yet to address your spending and financial habit, then debt consolidation may be a huge mistake because you are yet to address the root cause of the

problem that got you into debt in the first place
- If you can't do without your credit card, then debt consolidation may be a banana peel for you.

Is Debt Consolidation A Good Idea In Your Situation?

Getting approved for debt consolidation doesn't mean that it is the wisest choice. As seen from above, there are situations which are favourable for debt consolidation, and there are times when you should not even bother consolidating your debt. The key is clarifying your financial goal. Browse and research for alternatives and pay attention to your overall interest rate, not just your monthly payments. Put a timeline on when you want to be free of debt. Plus, some unscrupulous lenders will approve you for debt consolidation even with bad credit. This can plunge you deeper into debt because you took out a loan you couldn't afford.

HOW ASSETS AND LIABILITIES AFFECT YOU WHEN PURCHASING REAL ESTATE

Buying a home takes a huge financial commitment, and may be the most significant financial decision that you may take. Still, the prices if homes is far beyond the reach of the average person, as such many people need to take out loans in other to purchase their house.

To determine your financial capability, lenders examine a lot of areas before they make a mortgage offer. They try to create a complete picture of your financial situation. This is why when you apply for a mortgage loan, you are asked to list your assets and liabilities. This information is used to assess your financial capability to repay the loan.

Assets And Real Estate Purchase

The word "asset" refers to anything that is useful or holds present or future value. You can list your liquid or illiquid assets in your prequalification form. Liquid assets are those assets that can be converted to cash easily. These include your savings and checking accounts, certificates of deposit, monetary gifts, retirement accounts like 401(k)s and individual retirement arrangements, and portfolios of stocks, bonds and mutual funds. Illiquid assets are assets which can't be converted to cash easily. These include things like your business, real estate property, cars or personal items of value. Because they're illiquid, lenders place less emphasis on this type of asset.

Liabilities And Real Estate Purchase

Liabilities are debts that are owed. They may be revolving or non-revolving. Of the two, lenders pay particular attention to your revolving debt over your non-revolving debt. In mortgage applications, liabilities are car loans, student loans, alimony, credit card debt and other mortgages.

The financial coats of your liabilities determine the amount you would be offered and the interest rate. The amount of liability you have impacts on your debt-to-income ratio, which invariably determines your eligibility for a mortgage. The higher your debt, the lower the amount of mortgage you qualify for, and the higher your interest rate.

Revolving liabilities affect mortgage qualification the most. Two of the most significant liabilities that home buyers are faced with are revolving liabilities - *Student Loans and Car loans.* Student loan makes it difficult to save money for a down payment. Missing a student loan payment can lower your credit score. If deferred for more than 12 months, such loans are illegible for exemption from FHA, VA and Conventional Loans. Car payments, on the other hand, are high due to having shorter amortization schedules. The Average auto monthly payments are $400 per month. This is equivalent to an $80,000 mortgage.

Liabilities increase your risk, which means lenders would find it less desirable to offer you a mortgage. Even if you have a lot of savings, if your debt exceeds your assets and income, your lender would be worried that you can't pay. This is because you would not have sufficient mortgage reserves to take care of your mortgage payments.

Debt-To-Income Ratio

Having liabilities doesn't mean you don't qualify for a mortgage. Lenders use various means to evaluate your financial situation. One of the most essential tools which lenders use to access your financial situation is the debt is the Debt to income ratio. A good DTI to get approved for a mortgage is 36%. Use our DTI calculator to find yours. A high DTI could result to higher interest rates or outright denial of a loan request.

Your debt-to-income ratio, or DTI, plays a large role in whether you're ready and able to qualify for a mortgage. It's the percentage of your income that goes toward paying your monthly debts, and it helps lenders decide how much you can borrow. DTI is as vital as your credit score and job stability, if not more so.

This gives them a comprehensive picture of your financial status and ability to pay the mortgage. Lenders use it as a measure of your ability to repay the money you have borrowed or to take on additional debt. DTI can be calculated by adding your monthly debts and dividing the sum by your monthly income.

Improve Your Chances

As seen from above, your assets and liabilities have implications on your ability to our side a home. It tells the lender your risk value which is evaluated using the debt to income ratio. Having assets increased one's chances of obtaining a reduced mortgage at a lower interest rate. This does not mean that having debts would disqualify you outrightly. But be prepared to pay higher interest rates for low loans. As such, it is advisable to build up your seats and pay off your debts two months prior to applying for a mortgage of you want to get reasonable rates.

CALCULATING YOUR MORTGAGE

Understanding the numbers behind your mortgage works enables you to make better financial decisions. Just like any loan application, you have to scrutinize the numbers and percentages unless you would run into a financial impasse.

One thing you have to take cognisance of is that when making your monthly mortgage payment, you're not just paying off the price of the home. Your payment includes principal, interest, taxes, and insurance – plus a few extra costs. People tend to overlook these costs and focus on the monthly payment when drawing up budgets, which can lead to surprises.

What Does A Mortgage Payment Include?

There are various costs which coalesce to form your mortgage. The individual costs all impact on your monthly payments. These are:

- **Principal:** This is the amount you borrowed. You could refer to it as the initial capital. Whenever you make a payment, it reduces the principal you owe.
- **Interest**: This is what you are charged for borrowing money. Interest rates are expressed as an annual percentage and can be calculated monthly.
- **Property taxes:** This is tax paid on your property and land to the government. This is included in your monthly mortgage payment, which your service provider saves in an escrow account and remits to the gov-

ernment when the taxes are due.
- **Homeowners insurance:** Mortgages come with insurance policies which cover damages to your home, or injury on the property. This is also included in your monthly mortgage payment which afterwards is remitted to the government by your loan service provider when due.
- **Private Mortgage Insurance**: If you make a down payment of less than 20% of the home's value, you'll be required to pay mortgage insurance. This protects the lender's interest against defaults on the mortgage by the borrower. Once you own 20% home equity, the mortgage insurance is cancelled, unless you have an FHA loan.

You can calculate your mortgage payment by simply using an online calculator. However, if you love to crunch numbers want to see how all of the variables work on the fly, you can do this manually using the mortgage monthly payment formula.

<u>How To Calculate Monthly Mortgage Payments Manually</u>.

It's also possible to estimate a mortgage payment by hand by using the following formula to find the principal and interest:

$M = P[r(1+r)^n/((1+r)^n-1)]$.

Where:

M = Monthly mortgage payment.

P = Principal loan amount.

r = Interest rate

n = Number of monthly payments

For example:

You buy a property priced at $150,000 and make a 10% ($15,000) down payment for a 30-year fixed-rate mortgage with at 4% interest rate.

Using the formula: $M = P[r(1+r)^n/((1+r)^n - 1)]$.

Where:

P = $135,000

r = 0.003333

n = 360

When the figures are plugged in:

M = $135,000[0.003333(1+0.003333)^360/((1+0.003333)^360 - 1]$

M = $135,000[0.00477392237]

M = $644.48

You can always cross-check your final figure using a Loan Amortization Calculator spreadsheet.

Why You Need to Calculate Your Mortgage

Knowing how to calculate your mortgage can help you make appropriate decisions when considering a home. If you do calculate manually or use tools, calculating your mortgage, bring clarity to judgments affecting your financial decisions, and puts into context how much impact the mortgage would have on your present financial status. Some issues it helps you clarify are:

To know if the loan affordable

Knowing how to calculate your mortgage enables you to answer a crucial question: how much house can I afford? Before applying for a mortgage, it is necessary to have a review of your income and monthly expenses. This clarifies your financial standing and liquidity in terms of how much you can afford to part with monthly as mortgage payment. Lenders generally offer the largest loan you are qualified for using based on their standards for an acceptable debt-to-income ratio. However, borrowing less than the maximum available is an indication of good financial acumen. This gives some you wiggle room each month in case you need to take care of other emergencies.

To know how much of the house you own

Of course, the house is yours— that's until it's fully paid for. Until then, the lender has an interest, or a lien, on the property. As such, it is important to understand how much home equity you control. You can get this value by subtracting your outstanding loan balance from the current market value of 'your' home. The ratio between these two variables is known as your loan-to-value (LTV) ratio. This is what lenders use to estimate how much loan you qualify for. LTV ratio is also useful if you want to borrow against your home using second mortgages and home equity lines of credit (HELOCs).

To have a clearer picture

Calculating your mortgage also helps you keep your spending in check. It gives you a wakeup call on how much you can pay each month, especially when other costs and taxes are considered. It also prevents you from putting in too little money, especially when you can get minimum down payments as low as 3%.

To figure out ways to reduce payments and interests

Calculating your mortgage helps you figure out a way to reduce your payments and interests. It lets you know how far you can stretch the tenure of the loan without hurting your balance sheet.

Reduce Your Monthly Payment With These Strategies

There are specific ways you can reduce your monthly payments on mortgages

Reduce the loan tenor

It pays to put the big picture in perspective. While it is good to keep an eye on monthly payments, you should not also lose sight of what the cost would amount to in years. A longer-term loan such as (30-year loans) would make your monthly payment lower, but you'll pay more interest over the years. Loans that are short-termed like 15-year mortgages often have lower rates. You may pay bigger instalments monthly, buy you would spend less on interest and overall amount. Plus you reduce the time it takes you to own the home.

Go for a cheaper house.

You can also reduce your monthly payment by going for a cheaper house. A cheaper house means a smaller loan, which invariably implies less interest to pay.

Make a larger down payment

Making a larger down payment reduces your interest rate. Your down payment determines your loan deficit on, which is then used to calculate your monthly instalment when the interest and other costs are factored in. A large down payment reduces the deficit, which reduces your monthly instalments. Also, large down payments help you avoid paying for Private Mortgage Insurance too. That means a lower monthly mortgage payment. A down payment of 20% or more, means you have at least 20% equity in the home lets you avoid PMI when you refinance.

Pay extra each month.

You can also reduce your mortgage payments when you make extra payments each month. Each time you make an extra payment on your mortgage, it reduces to your principal balance. However, it is advisable you check with your company first before making any extra payments. Some companies only accept extra payments at specific times. Moreso, they may charge prepayment penalties. When making an extra payment, you can include a note that you want it applied to the principal balance, not the following month's payment.

When Can Your Monthly Payment Go Up?

Mortgage payment schedules are not cast in gold but reflect the prevailing economic conditions. There are certain times which your mortgage payments can increase:

- When there is a rise in property taxes, or homeowners, insurance premiums rise. These costs are reflected in most mortgage payments.
- When you incur fees due to late payment to your service provider.
- If you operate an adjustable-rate mortgage, your rate may rise at the adjustment period.

HOW TO FIND THE BEST REAL ESTATE AGENT, LOAN OFFICER AND MORTGAGE BROKER

Real estate markets in most countries are not as organized or efficient as other markets with liquid investment instruments. Real estate properties tend unique and directly interchangeable among themselves. This presents a significant challenge for an investor seeking investment opportunities in this asset class.

For this reason, locating properties which to buy or sell, including the resources to finance it, can involve substantial effort. One way to wriggle around this is to seek the services of a mortgage broker, real estate agent or loan coordinator. These agents have their ear to the ground as such could be a reliable source of the best real estate deals.

However, though there are numerous mortgage brokers and real estate agents, finding a reliable one that understands our needs tends to be few and far between. This has bungled the hopes of many investors hoping to takes a bite of real estate investments.

We have decided to compile a list of tips that can help you find the best real estate agent, mortgage broker or loan officer. Though the steps required are primarily the same, each category presents its unique search parameters.

Real Estate Agent

Real estate agents are licensed professionals that arrange transactions between real estate buyers and sellers together and acts as their representatives during the course of negotiations. Real estate agents are compensated through commissions on the property's purchase price; as such, their income is tied to their ability to get a deal closed.

How To Find The Best Real Estate Agent

Research

Any venture into unknown territory begins with research. There are various ways to search for a real estate gnat. You can go online and search directories. Browse through websites and social media accounts of realtors that pop up in your search radar. Be sure to read online reviews as this would give you an indication of how efficient the real estate agent is. Alternatively, you can check with your state's real estate regulator for background information.

Referrals

Referrals are a tried and tested method of getting good real estate agents. This is because you have the opportunity to evaluate their efficiency first hand. Also, because looking for a suitable property requires a bit of knack, you would want someone who has experience working with clients who have similar needs such as yours. You can ask friends, family or colleagues for recommendations. Ideally, it would be best if you searched for a real estate agent that's a member of the National Association of Realtors (NAR) and or certified realtors.

Set up an interview

An interview allows you to evaluate the agent close up. Apart from his experience, you would also be looking at his mannerism and character. Interviews give you a chance to know if what the agent is offering aligns with your needs. It also helps you trash out the mode of communication and commissions. During the interview process, you can ask prospective agents to provide information on homes they've listed and sold in the past year. You can do a follow-up by calling those clients and asking for their opinions on the agent and find out if they would hire him again given similar circumstances.

Keep an eye on commissions.

Before closing the deal or signing the dotted lines, it is imperative that you get an idea of how much commission your agent is making off the deal—ideally, a 6% commission of the sales price of the home.

Loan Officer

Loan officers are mainly concerned with the financial side of obtaining a mortgage. They are different from real estate agents who are primarily involved with connecting buyers and sellers. Though some real estate agent also follow up mortgage financing options, knowing which loan best suits your financial situation is within the prerogative of the loan officer. A loan officer can help you make sound decisions regarding your mortgage. One advantage of working with a loan officer is that it removes the presence of a middle man, making it possible to speed up the process of a loan application.

How to find the best loan officer

Know your lending options

Knowing what options for that are available for lending automatically crosses-out what type of lenders are unsuitable for you.

Know that there are different types of mortgage lenders available each which their unique advantages and disadvantages. Credit unions, mortgage bankers, correspondent lenders and Savings and Loans (S&L) are some of the available mortgage lenders. One significant parameter which is used to find the most suitable loan officer is the interest rate. Locking in a low-interest rate is critical, but be careful that there are no hidden charges which could affect your purse.

Work on your credit rating

A loan officer provides finance for the purchase of a home. This is highly predicated on your credit score. Typically, a loan officer would evaluate your financial circumstance and ability to repay to determine if you are eligible for the loan. A low credit rating implies that you are a risky candidate which attracts a higher interest rate. The higher your credit rating implies that you are a low-risk candidate who has the ability to pay. This does not only attract a lower interest rate but also increases your negotiating power and expands the scope of your search for a good loan officer.

Compare

This stage occurs after you must have researched and asked for referrals (as outlined in the real estate agent section). You then compare and contrast the best lending rates available. This information can also be used as leverage when negotiating with lenders.

Interview

Follow the process outlined in the real estate agent section.

Mortgage Broker

Mortgage brokers work as intermediaries between lenders and borrowers. Because they are not tied to a single lender, mortgage brokers can shop around for the best rates and mortgages, though they may favour one lender over another because of the commissions they receive. However, a good broker should look out for his client's interests above anything else.

How To Find The Best Mortgage Broker

The steps to finding a good mortgage broker have been outlined in the previous section. This includes asking for referrals, researching, conducting interviews and background checks comparing rates with different brokers. You could also expand the radius of your search to include brokers not listed in your area.

CONCLUSION

Debts can sometimes cause our lives to be unsettling and cause us to be nervy. It also hampers our ability to save and invest, which implies putting our future at risk. There are various ways to tackle debt. You can use one or a combination of the outlined strategies to manage your debt effectively. The starting point is recognizing that you need to manage your debt and taking appropriate steps to achieve this. The earlier you start, the sooner you break the cycle of debt. The price of being debt free is lower than been indebted. Take care!

BOOKS BY THIS AUTHOR

Tackling Gaming Disorder: How Parents Can Help Their Kids Deal With Video Game Addiction

This book spotlights on the effects of video games, how parents can spot symptoms of video game addiction and approaches they can take to help their kids. It looks at why kids are addicted to video games, how video games can be beneficial and strategies of how parents can prevent and treat their kids.

How To Host Virtual Meetings: Visual Etiquette In A Digital Economy

The advent of the novel coronavirus has altered the way we work. more than ever, humans are depending on technology to execute tasks and permeate their existence as social beings. With the rise of remote working, virtual meetings are fast becoming the new reality. Just like offline events, preparing an online conference can be just as tasking. How to Host Virtual Meetings spotlights on ways remote workers and corporations can effectively organize meetings from the comfort of their homes without missing a beat. it suggests tools, etiquette and strategies of making your virtual meetings fun and entertaining, yet informative.

Taking The Dope Out Of Dopamine

This books takes a deep dive into the chemical responsible for our addictive behaviors. It demystifies the chemical, dopamine, and how it makes us craving for more and pushes the threshold of our satisfaction. it includes unhealthy triggers of dopamine such as pornography, masturbation and alcoholism. it suggests healthy ways we can lower our dopamine and reduce our cravings. it is a must for anyone dealing with an addiction.

Healthy Ways Of Working From Home

Working from home is the new reality - a fact has made more obvious following the global pandemic which has forced us to alter our lives. They way we work has significantly changed due to technology. and the growth of the gig economy. As we embrace remote working, this raises questions about its effects on several aspects of our health. This books looks at healthy ways we can work from home without mortgaging our health. it looks at physical, mental and social aspects of our health. it also includes a chapter on how to eat healthy when working from home. it is a must read for every remote worker.

www.ingramcontent.com/pod-product-compliance
Lightning Source LLC
Chambersburg PA
CBHW070500220526
45466CB00004B/1907